Military and Elite Forces Officer

CAREERS WITH CHARACTER

Careers with Character

Military and Elite Forces Officer

by Joyce Libal

MASON CREST PUBLISHERS

Mason Crest Publishers Inc.
370 Reed Road, Broomall, Pennsylvania 19008
(866) MCP-BOOK (toll free)
www.masoncrest.com

First edition, 2003
13 12 11 10 09 08 07 06 05 04   10 9 8 7 6 5 4 3 2

Library of Congress Cataloging-in-Publication Data

Libal, Joyce.
  Military and elite forces officer / by Joyce Libal.
      v. cm.—(Careers with character)
Includes bibliographical references and index.
Contents: Job requirements—Integrity and trustworthiness—Respect and
compassion—Justice and fairness—Responsibility—Courage—Self-discipline and
diligence—Citizenship—Career opportunities.
  ISBN   1-59084-318-5
            1-59084-327-4 (series)
1. United States—Armed Forces—Officers—Vocational guidance—Juvenile
literature. [1. United States—Armed Forces—Officers—Vocational guidance. 2.
Vocational guidance.] I. Title. II. Series.
  UB413.L53 2003
  355'.0023'73—dc21
                              2002154667

Produced by Harding House Publishing Service, www.hardinghousepages.com
Design by Lori Holland.
Composition by Byteway Publishing Services, Binghamton, New York.
Printed in the Hashemite Kingdom of Jordan.

CONTENTS

v

We each leave a fingerprint on the world.
Our careers are the work we do in life.
Our characters are shaped by the choices
we make to do good.
When we combine careers with character,
we touch the world with power.

INTRODUCTION

by Dr. Cheryl Gholar
and Dr. Ernestine G. Riggs

In today's world, the awesome task of choosing or staying in a career has become more involved than one would ever have imagined in past decades. Whether the job market is robust or the demand for workers is sluggish, the need for top-performing employees with good character remains a priority on most employers' lists of "must have" or "must keep." When critical decisions are being made regarding a company or organization's growth or future, job performance and work ethic are often the determining factors as to who will remain employed and who will not.

How does one achieve success in one's career and in life? Victor Frankl, the Austrian psychologist, summarized the concept of success in the preface to his book *Man's Search for Meaning* as: "The unintended side-effect of one's personal dedication to a course greater than oneself." Achieving value by responding to life and careers from higher levels of knowing and being is a specific goal of teaching and learning in "Careers with Character." What constitutes success for us as individuals can be found deep within our belief system. Seeking, preparing, and attaining an excellent career that aligns with our personality is an outstanding goal. However, an excellent career augmented by exemplary character is a visible expression of the human need to bring meaning, purpose, and value to our work.

Career education informs us of employment opportunities, occupational outlooks, earnings, and preparation needed to perform certain

1

tasks. Character education provides insight into how a person of good character might choose to respond, initiate an action, or perform specific tasks in the presence of an ethical dilemma. "Careers with Character" combines the two and teaches students that careers are more than just jobs. Career development is incomplete without character development. What better way to explore careers and character than to make them a single package to be opened, examined, and reflected upon as a means of understanding the greater whole of who we are and what work can mean when one chooses to become an employee of character?

Character can be defined simply as "who you are even when no one else is around." Your character is revealed by your choices and actions. These bear your personal signature, validating the story of who you are. They are the fingerprints you leave behind on the people you meet and know; they are the ideas you bring into reality. Your choices tell the world what you truly believe.

Character, when viewed as a standard of excellence, reminds us to ask ourselves when choosing a career: "Why this particular career, for what purpose, and to what end?" The authors of "Careers with Character" knowledgeably and passionately, through their various vignettes, enable one to experience an inner journey that is both intellectual and moral. Students will find themselves, when confronting decisions in real life, more prepared, having had experiential learning opportunities through this series. The books, however, do not separate or negate the individual good from the academic skills or intellect needed to perform the required tasks that lead to productive career development and personal fulfillment.

Each book is replete with exemplary role models, practical strategies, instructional tools, and applications. In each volume, individuals of character work toward ethical leadership, learning how to respond appropriately to issues of not only right versus wrong, but issues of right versus right, understanding the possible benefits and consequences of their decisions. A wealth of examples is provided.

What is it about a career that moves our hearts and minds toward fulfilling a dream? It is our character. The truest approach to finding out who we are and what illuminates our lives is to look within. At the very heart of career development is good character. At the heart of good character is an individual who knows and loves the good, and seeks to share the good with others. By exploring careers and character together, we create internal and external environments that support and enhance each other, challenging students to lead conscious lives of personal quality and true richness every day.

Is there a difference between doing the right thing, and doing things right? Career questions ask, "What do you know about a specific career?" Character questions ask, "Now that you know about a specific career, what will you choose to do with what you know?" "How will you perform certain tasks and services for others, even when no one else is around?" "Will all individuals be given your best regardless of their socioeconomic background, physical condition, ethnicity, or religious beliefs?" Character questions often challenge the authenticity of what we say we believe and value in the workplace and in our personal lives.

Character and career questions together challenge us to pay attention to our lives and not fall asleep on the job. Career knowledge, self-knowledge, and ethical wisdom help us answer deeper questions about the meaning of work; they give us permission to transform our lives. Personal integrity is the price of admission.

The insight of one "ordinary" individual can make a difference in the world—if that one individual believes that character is an amazing gift to uncap knowledge and talents to empower the human community. Our world needs everyday heroes in the workplace—and "Careers with Character" challenges students to become those heroes.

This statue in Gallipoli, Turkey, commemorates the character of World War II soldiers.

1

JOB REQUIREMENTS

*The military asks a lot . . . but it
also gives a lot back.*

Colin Powell was born in Harlem in 1937 to parents who had immi-grated from Jamaica. They moved to the United States dreaming of a bright future for themselves and their children. Drugs, crime, and poverty plagued the neighborhood of Colin's youth, but Powell credits his parents for the strong upbringing he had despite that. His mother was a seamstress, and his father worked for a shipping company. Some may consider their employment humble, but Mr. and Mrs. Powell brought sustenance and dignity into their home and had high expecta-tions for their children. Powell says his parents provided him with, "a set of core beliefs, a value system founded on a clear understanding of the difference between right and wrong. . . ." Powell's parents taught him that "Integrity and kindness were doctrines that were right—lying, crime, violence, intolerance, drugs were wrong, and even worse than wrong in my family—they were shameful!"

Being raised in New York enabled Colin to interact with people of many ethnic origins, different backgrounds, and various religions. As an African American growing up in the 1940s and '50s, Colin did expe-rience racism, but his parents countered those situations with common sense and good advice.

Although Colin's elementary and high school career cannot be

If you are thinking about enlisting in the military:

- Learn about military life before making a decision.
- Speak to friends and relatives about their military experiences.
- Determine what the military can offer you and what it will expect in return.
- Talk to a recruiter who can:
  1) determine if you qualify for enlistment;
  2) explain the various enlistment options;
  3) tell you which military occupational specialties currently have openings.

considered a rousing academic success, he did maintain a C average and was able to enroll in the City College of New York. There he entered the Army Reserve Officers Training Corps (ROTC), a decision that forever changed his life. Colin thrived in the structure, discipline, and camaraderie of the military. He received his bachelor's degree in 1958 and attained the rank of second lieutenant.

Powell did encounter segregation in the Army, but self-assurance and strength of character helped him overcome unfairness. Powell learned from every situation he encountered. Experiences in Vietnam taught him

If you are considering a career in the military, find out what to expect. Are the demands of the military a good match to your personality and character?

The U.S. Army uses Apache attack helicopters during battle.

that each military action should have a clearly defined purpose. He returned to the United States a hero, having survived a helicopter crash where he saved three soldiers. Powell moved to Washington, D.C., married, and returned to school. This time he earned straight As at George Washington University and the National War College. Colin Powell served his country in several posts and accumulated many military awards. He served several U.S. Presidents and, after being a career soldier, became a diplomat.

- During President Gerald Ford's administration, Powell was accepted into the White House Fellows Program.
- Under President Ronald Reagan, Powell became Deputy National Security Adviser and later the first African American named National Security Adviser.
- President George Bush appointed him to the highest military rank in the nation, Chairman of the Joint Chiefs of Staff (the top military advisor to the President).

An officer's accomplishments are the result of experience, training, and character.

Armed Services Vocational Aptitude Battery

All prospective recruits are required to take this exam. The recruiter can schedule it for you without any obligation. Many schools offer the exam as an easy way for students to explore the possibility of a military career. The test also provides insight into nonmilitary career areas in which a student has demonstrated aptitudes and interests. The military uses this test as a placement exam, and test scores largely determine an individual's chances of being accepted into a particular training program.

- President Bill Clinton asked Powell to chair America's Promise, a civic organization dedicated to uplifting youth through mentoring programs, after-school programs, and education.
- President George W. Bush appointed Colin Powell Secretary of State.

Colin Powell's accomplishments are a result of his military experiences, other life experiences, and strong character.

The military offers men and women of all races and religions diverse opportunities for satisfying careers. Whatever your interests, if you're the kind of person who is trusted and respected by your peers, if you have demonstrated a sense of responsibility at your school, if you treat others with fairness and compassion, there is a place for you in one of the branches of the military.

The military classifies its members as either "enlisted" or "officers." Requirements for each branch of the military vary, but certain qualifications are common to all of them. In order to enlist in the U.S. military, one must be between 17 and 35 years old, be a U.S. citizen or immigrant alien holding permanent resident status, not have a felony record, and possess a birth certificate. Applicants who are 17 must have the consent of a parent or legal guardian before entering the service.

All branches of the Armed Forces require high school graduation or its equivalent for certain enlistment options. Courses designed to help

Basic Training

Following enlistment, new members of the Armed Forces undergo recruit training, better known as "basic training." Basic training provides a six- to 12-week introduction to military life with courses in military skills and protocol. Days and nights are carefully structured and include rigorous physical exercise designed to improve strength and endurance and to build a sense of camaraderie among members of the unit.

Officers

Officer training in the U.S. Armed Forces is provided through:

- Federal Service Academies (Military, Naval, Air Force, and Coast Guard)
- Reserve Officers Training Corps (ROTC) offered at many colleges and universities
- Officer Candidate School (OCS) or Officer Training School (OTS)
- National Guard (State Officer Candidate School Programs)
- Uniformed Services University of Health Science, and other programs.

All are selective and are good options for those wishing to make the military a career. Persons interested in attending the Federal Service Academies must be single to enter and graduate. Those seeking training through OCS, OTS, and ROTC need not be single. Single parents with one or more minor dependents are not eligible for officer commissioning.

---

personnel earn high school equivalency diplomas are available. Applicants must pass a written examination, called the Armed Services Vocational Aptitude Battery, must meet certain minimum physical standards, and sign an enlistment contract. Negotiating the contract involves choosing, qualifying, and agreeing on a number of items including length of active duty time. Most active duty programs have first-term enlistments of four years, although there are some two-, three-, and six-year programs. Depending on the terms of the contract, two to six years are spent on active duty, and the balance is spent in the reserves. The enlistment contract obligates the service to provide the agreed-upon job, rating, pay, cash bonuses for enlistment in certain occupations, medical and other benefits, occupational training, and continuing education. In return, enlisted personnel must serve satisfactorily for the period of time specified. A Non-Commissioned Member (NCM) of the Canadian Forces serves three years, while Canadian Officers serve nine years.

All branches of the U.S. military offer a "delayed entry program." Active duty can be delayed for up to one year after enlisting. High school students can, therefore, enlist during their senior year and enter service after graduation. Others may choose this option because the job training they desire is not immediately available but will be accessible within the coming year or because they need time to arrange personal matters.

All new U.S. *recruits* participate in basic training. Following that, most take additional training at technical schools that prepare them for a particular occupational specialty. Training generally lasts from ten to 20 weeks. For certain occupations it can take as long as a year. Recruits not assigned to classroom instruction receive on-the-job training at their first duty assignment.

Recruits participate in basic training before they are assigned to active duty.

Federal Service Academies

These institutions provide a four-year college program leading to a bachelor of science degree. Midshipmen and cadets are provided with free room and board, tuition, medical and dental care, and a monthly allowance. Graduates receive regular or reserve commissions and have a five-year active duty obligation, more if they enter flight school.

An authorized source, usually a Congressperson, must provide a nomination for a candidate to the service academies. Nominees must have an academic record of the requisite quality, college aptitude test scores above an established minimum, recommendations from teachers or school officials, and must pass a medical examination. Appointments are made from the list of eligible nominees. Appointments to the Coast Guard Academy are based strictly on merit and do not require a nomination.

In addition to on-duty training, military personnel may choose from a variety of educational programs. Some receive college credit for the technical training they receive on duty which, combined with off-duty courses, can lead to a degree. Most military installations have tuition assistance programs for people wishing to take courses during off-duty hours. These may be correspondence courses or degree programs offered by local colleges and universities. Tuition assistance pays up to 75 percent of college costs. Each service branch provides opportunities for full-time study to a limited number of exceptional applicants. Military personnel accepted into these competitive programs receive full pay, allowances, tuition, and related fees. In return, they agree to serve an additional amount of time in the service. Other selective programs enable enlisted personnel to qualify as commissioned officers through additional military training. Canadian citizens, too, can earn college degrees while simultaneously working in the Canadian Forces, and there is also a military university in Canada known as the Royal Military College.

General Colin Powell says, "The beautiful part about the army is that they were always giving me something that was beyond me. They were always testing me. And by being pushed, I grew fast." Do you enjoy a physical and mental challenge? When you do your schoolwork or other types of work, are you committed to doing the best job possible?

ROTC

You'll gain self-confidence, motivation, leadership skills, and management skills in the Reserve Officers Training Corps. ROTC requires two to five hours of time each week while in college. ROTC trains students in about 950 Army, 67 Navy and Marine Corps, and 1,000 Air Force units at participating colleges and universities. According to the ROTC web site, you can try it for two years without obligation, and scholarships are available to qualifying students. In the last two years of an ROTC program, students receive a monthly allowance while attending school and additional pay for summer training.

Classwork involves: 1) history, structure, and functions of the military, and 2) how to think and act like a leader including organizing tasks, making decisions, and using time efficiently. Presentation skills training and a Cadet writing program are included. Field exercises and physical training teach how to set goals and achieve them. Hands-on exercises such as land navigation and platoon tactics help individuals develop judgment and decisiveness. Upon graduation you'll use your training while serving on active duty or part time in the Reserves or National Guard.

Ranks and Promotions

Each branch of the military has different ranks for its members and criteria for promoting them. Promotion criteria may include time in service and grade, job performance, a fitness report (supervisor's recommendation), and written examinations.

Would you like to dedicate a portion of your life to the service of your country? Whatever your ethnic, financial, or educational background, consider the benefits of a military commitment.

The U.S. Military has five branches: Army, Navy, Air Force, Marines, and Coast Guard. The Canadian Military has three branches: Army, Navy, and Air Force. The ma-

Officer Candidate Schools and Officer Training Schools

College graduates can earn a commission in the Armed Forces through OCS or OTS programs. These officers generally serve their obligation on active duty. Those training in certain health professions may qualify for direct appointment as officers as well as financial assistance and internship opportunities in return for specified periods of military service. Prospective medical students can apply to the Uniformed Services University of Health Sciences, which offers free tuition in a program leading to a Doctor of Medicine (M.D.) degree. In return, graduates must serve for seven years in either the military or the U.S. Public Health Service. Direct appointments also are available for those qualified to serve in other specialty areas, such as the judge advocate general (legal) or chaplain corps. Flight training is available to commissioned officers in each branch of the Armed Forces. In addition, the Army has a direct enlistment option to become a warrant officer aviator.

jor requirement for military service is strength of character, including trustworthiness, respect, responsibility, fairness, caring, and citizenship. If you possess these traits, a career in the military may interest you—and could lead to successful civilian employment as well.

There is no secret formula for success. Success simply requires a clear goal and a genuine commitment to do the very best job you know how.

—Colin Powell

Planes like this one were used in the Battle of Britain during World War II.

2

INTEGRITY AND TRUSTWORTHINESS

Selfish concerns can prompt us to tell lies—but concern for others prompts us to tell the truth.

Genevieve's earliest memory was of the songs of birds. She was only four years old when she heard the lovely sound, looked up toward the heavens, and longed to fly. Her parents were charmed by the young child's arm-flapping antics as they watched her chasing robins in the yard.

In primary school the story of the Wright brothers' first flight fascinated her. Charles Lindbergh was her hero. Proudly displaying the small model her father helped her build of Lindbergh's *Spirit of St. Louis*, she told her classmates of Lindbergh's trans-Atlantic flight. Perhaps it was strange for a girl growing up in the 1980s, but it wasn't long before becoming a pilot in the Royal Canadian Air Force became the preeminent thought in the mind of Genevieve Villenauve. Genevieve held true to her ambition throughout secondary school, and it grew as she did. "I feel so blessed," she shared with friends who were uncertain of their own futures. "I know how lucky I am to already realize the thing that I was born to do."

Gen's parents were proud of her unceasing ambition. Her grand-

World War II fighter planes were brightly decorated.

father Edward was a retired pilot who had participated in the Battle of Britain during World War II. Grandfather Ed was an exceptional story-teller, so the battle raged vividly in Genevieve's mind as her grandfather relived it. "More than 100 Canadian pilots flew on fighter operations during the Battle of Britain, and of course many more served on the ground crew," he would always begin. Gen knew from her studies that it was the first time since the inception of the Royal Canadian Air Force in 1924 that Canadian airmen flew in Canadian units in a sustained battle. Genevieve's mind was alive with the sounds, sights, and even the smells of battle as Ed recounted his harrowing adventure. It was frightening, but it filled her heart with excited beats as she imagined the adrenaline of battle.

After secondary school, Genevieve studied aviation technology at a local community college. The classes were interesting and enjoyable because Gen knew she was making progress toward reaching her ultimate goal, but time can pass slowly when a goal is as clearly defined as Genevieve's had been for so many years. By her last year at the college she could no longer wait to lift her body from the confines of the earth. After much convincing, her parents allowed her to take skydiving lessons at a small local airport. Genevieve loved and respected her parents. They always understood and supported the drive and commitment she felt. The fact that they allowed her to add this exhilarating activity to her life made her feelings for them even stronger.

The excitement Genevieve felt as she conquered fear and stepped out of the plane was intoxicating. Every dive was more wonderful than the last. She loved the feel of air surrounding her body as she sailed high above land and water, above human concerns, above the problems of life, above all life forms save the birds—the lucky, beautiful birds that could truly fly.

After graduation Genevieve began Basic Officer Training and Second Language Training at Saint-Jean, Quebec. Soon she would begin the Basic Flying Course in Winnipeg, Manitoba. Gen's life was really on track when the most curious and unexpected event took place. One night, just like any other, Genevieve went to sleep. But late in the evening Gen's life was forever changed when she awoke to the sound and surprise of her own arm flailing away from her body and hitting the bedroom wall. The really

People who value integrity and trustworthiness:

- tell the truth.
- don't withhold important information.
- are sincere; they don't deceive, mislead, try to trick others.
- don't betray a trust.
- don't steal.
- don't cheat.
- stand up for beliefs about right and wrong.
- keep their promises.
- return what they have borrowed and pay their debts.
- support and protect their families, friends, community, and country.
- don't talk behind people's backs or spread rumors.
- don't ask their friends to do something wrong.

Adapted from material from the Character Counts Coalition, 4640 Admiralty Way, Suite 1001, Marina del Rey, California 90292.

curious thing was that she couldn't stop it. After a few seconds it stopped on its own, and Genevieve went back to sleep. If only it had ended there, Genevieve could have proceeded with her plans and dreams unscathed. But a week later it happened again, and then again, and again. And it grew worse. Gen suspected she was having *seizures* because sometimes she woke up confused, and it was obvious that at some point during the night she had bitten her tongue.

Genevieve continued to make progress in her basic training and second language courses to the delight of her parents and her grandfather, but inside she was in turmoil. She had not spoken with her family about her health. Genevieve knew that she needed to have a physical examination by a doctor, and she was frightened to tell him about her medical condition. What if it meant she would never be able to realize

The requirements for flying today's fighter jets are demanding; you need concentration, coordination, dexterity, and good physical health.

Oh, I have slipped the surly bonds of earth
And danced the skies on laughter-silvered wings;
Sunward I've climbed, and joined the
tumbling mirth
Of sun-split clouds—and done a
hundred things
You have not dreamed of—wheeled
and soared and swung
High in the sunlit silence.
Hovering there I've chased the
shouting wind along,
and flung my eager craft through
footless halls of air.
Up, up the long, delirious, burning
blue
I've topped the windswept heights
with easy grace
Where never lark, or even eagle flew.
And, while with silent, lifting mind
I've trod
the high untrespassed sanctity of space,
Put out my hand, and touched the face of God.

"High Flight" was written by 19-year-old Royal Canadian Air Force Pilot John Gillespie Magee, Jr. while he was serving in England in 1941. According to Magee, he "started composing it at 30,000 feet, inspired by the ecstasy of this experience." John Magee died in an air collision only months after composing the sonnet.

her dream to be a pilot? Would it be wrong to just not mention it? After all, she was perfectly healthy during the daytime. Did other people really have to know what sometimes happened when she slept? Would people be in danger if she kept this secret?

Consider these questions:

In the middle of World War II, on June 18, 1940, Winston Churchill offered these words of encouragement and challenge to the British troops:

The Battle of France is over. I expect that the Battle of Britain is about to begin. Upon this battle depends the survival of Christian civilization. Upon it depends our British life, and the long continuity of our institutions and our Empire. The whole fury and might of the enemy must very soon be turned on us. Hitler knows that he will have to break us in this island or lose the war. Let us therefore brace ourselves to our duties, and so bear ourselves that, if the British Empire and its Commonwealth last for a thousand years, men will still say, "This was their finest hour."

Courageous pilots fought the Battle of Britain in the air

How did I live today?
Thomas Shanks, S.J., Ph.D. Executive Director of the Markkula Center for Applied Ethics, recommends everyone ask themselves these five questions at the end of each day:

- Did I practice any virtues (e.g., integrity, honesty, compassion)?
- Did I do more good than harm?
- Did I treat others with dignity and respect?
- Was I fair and just?
- Was my community better because I was in it?
- Was I better because I was in my community?

What would you do if you were Genevieve?

Have you ever kept a secret because you were afraid of the consequences if you told?

If Genevieve was your friend and told you about her medical condition, what would you advise her to do?

What would you do?

Do you trust your parents enough to go to them with a serious problem?

Integrity means you're the same person on the outside that you are on the inside.

—June Michael Day

Soldiers need courage and strength—but they also need respect and compassion.

3

RESPECT AND COMPASSION

*Respect and compassion for others ask us
to look past the barriers that separate us.*

"L ive and let live." That was Jack Goldstein's motto. Jack was proud
of the fact that he had grown up in a tough New Jersey neighborhood. It meant that he too was tough. After all, he had survived.

Yup, he was a tough, Jersey, Jewish guy. Not that he was particularly
wedded to his religion. After all, it was something he was born with, not
something he had chosen, not something he had fought for or worked to
achieve. Sure, he dutifully placed his *yarmulke* upon his head before
meals, but that was out of respect for his parents. And he had long since
stopped complaining about going to the synagogue. It just wasn't worth
the arguments and the lectures about the *Holocaust*. On the surface he
felt like he was tired of hearing about it, but down deeper it saddened
him to hear about the suffering of his grandparents and of so many families. The way children had been torn from their parents and wives from
their husbands, the trains packed with people being treated so inhu-
manely, the starvation, the medical experiments, the torture, the death—
it made him feel helpless, and that was a feeling Jack just couldn't toler-
ate. Helpless was something he had worked his whole life not to feel.

Yes, the thing that Jack was most proud of was definitely the fact that
he was tough. Everyone in the neighborhood and school respected Jack.
They were afraid not to for Jack had an impressive presence. Early on

Jack learned the benefit of physical strength and actively pursued it. Weight training from an early age had molded his body in a way that gave Jack confidence, and boxing at the local boy's club had reinforced it.

People who value respect and compassion:

- are courteous and polite.
- are tolerant; they accept individual's differences.
- don't mistreat or make fun of anyone.
- don't use or take advantage of others.
- respect others' rights to make their own decisions.
- are sensitive to others' feelings.
- live by the Golden Rule. (They treat others the way they want to be treated.)
- help others.
- share what they have with others.
- do what they can to help those who are in trouble.
- forgive others.

Adapted from material from the Character Counts Coalition, 4640 Admiralty Way, Suite 1001, Marina del Rey, California 90292.

When Jack wasn't engaged in physical activities, he enjoyed an occasional movie, and military movies were his favorites. He admired the heroes depicted on screen and could imagine himself in their positions. He started reading books about all the major wars and studied the strategy of various battles. The military began to look more and more appealing to Jack. Someone had to be the strong one after all. Someone had to defend the innocent and make the world safe.

It came as no surprise to Jack's parents when, in his senior year of high school, he enlisted in the military. Shortly after graduation, Jack was off to basic training. It was like he had been preparing to be a soldier all his life. Jack thrived on the discipline and physical demands. He respected his officers and didn't mind taking orders.

It was 1999, and the North Atlantic Treaty Organization (NATO) had just begun a military campaign against the Federal Republic of Yugoslavia. Jack knew his training was important. Members of his unit kept abreast of the air war in Kosovo, and shared the news with each other. Whenever the term "ethnic cleansing" was used, referring to the treatment of ethnic Albanians by Serbs, Jack was reminded of the sto-

This Special Forces officer holds a MP-5 9-millimeter machine gun; he needs a strong character to ensure he uses his weapon with respect for human life.

ries of the Holocaust. It mattered not that he was Jewish and they were Muslim; Jack felt **empathy** for the Albanians. Stories of thousands of people fleeing toward the border, of looted homes and villages on fire, of atrocities against children and babies—Jack couldn't stand hearing about it anymore. He wanted to fight for these people. He wanted to be the good battling evil.

Jack hoped the United States would send ground troops into the war. He trained hard and seriously and relished the idea of testing that training in the field. But on June 9, the 78-day war ended when Milosevic agreed to allow a 50,000-member multinational "peace-keeping force" to enter Kosovo. Jack didn't know what to think when his unit was **deployed** as part of that mission. This was the last thing in the world he had expected. He thought of himself as a soldier, not a "peace-keeper." But Jack did his duty; he headed for a foreign land, which appeared to be both at war and at peace simultaneously.

After landing in Kosovo, his unit quickly went about its job of "keeping the peace." Jack's patrols remained relatively uneventful. The

Living your life with respect and compassion for others is not a new idea. In fact, the Golden Rule has a history that stretches back thousands of years:

- Around 500 B.C. Confucius said, "What you do not want done to yourself, do not do to others."
- In 325 B.C. Aristotle said, "We should behave to others as we wish others to behave to us."
- The Mahabharata (written around 200 B.C.) said, "Do nothing to your neighbors that you would not have them do later to you."
- In A.D. 33 or thereabouts Jesus said, "Do to others as you would have them do to you."

The Golden Rule is found in the scriptures of many religions.

presence of soldiers seemed to keep most people from engaging in destructive activity. Jack got to know one of the interpreters, who shared the personal stories of some of the villagers. The suffering of one Albanian in particular tore at Jack's heart. This man had sent his 12-year-old son out of the village along with his wife and daughters. They had traveled with a large group of refugees over dangerous territory to relative safety at the border. Without his parent's permission, the boy then left his mother's side and managed to return to the village to "fight with his father." During a confrontation, the boy was killed by a former neighbor.

Unknown to anyone, the man had been looking for the neighbor ever since. One night he found him.

Jack was on patrol and realized the seriousness of the situation immediately. The Serb was on the ground and the Albanian was above him with a makeshift club. During all the times that Jack thought about coming to this place, he never thought he'd find himself in the position of defending a Serb. Jack only had a second to decide whether to do his duty and keep the peace—or look the other way.

What should he do?

An officer makes an ethical judgment and decides not to obey an order:

Although Russia was a member of the NATO Partnership for Peace Program, because of their history with the former Yugoslavia, Russia suspended formal cooperation with NATO during the war in Kosovo. The Russians were eager to play some type of role in Kosovo, however, and on June 12, 1999, they took control of the airport in Pristina. U.S. General Wesley Clark, then operating as NATO's supreme European commander, ordered Lieutenant General Sir Michael Jackson, the British commander, to force the Russians from the airport. The British commander refused the order, saying, "It's not worth starting World War III."

Respect focuses on the moral obligation to honor the essential worth and dignity of the individual. Respect prohibits violence. We have no ethical duty to hold all people in high esteem or to admire them, but we are morally obligated to treat everyone with respect, regardless of who they are and what they have done. We have a responsibility to be the best we can be in all situations, even when dealing with unpleasant people.

From www.josephsoninstitute.org/MED/MED-6pillars.htm

Military personnel don't only fight—they also have important peacekeeping duties.

Canadians as Peacekeepers

"Peace Keeping first came about during the Suez Crisis of 1956," states Christopher Hovius of Queen's University in Kingston, Ontario. "The idea of UN Peacekeeping took root because of a brain-storming session between former Canadian prime minister (1963-1968) and Nobel Peace Prize laureate (1957) Lester B. Pearson and the Secretary General of the UN. At the time, Pearson was Minister of External Affairs in Canada, a position since renamed Minister of Foreign Affairs. Canada has participated in nearly every subsequent peacekeeping mission. The idea is to prevent war in conflicts that are at an intermediate stage between peace and war. The purpose is not to create peace, but rather the conditions necessary for the movement toward peace. In other words, to keep the situation from moving to the 'war extreme.' Canadian involvement is justified in that international peace and security are arguably necessary for Canadian peace and security."

It is better to suffer wrong than to do it.

—Samuel Johnson

Justice and fairness are important qualities in the military—but they probably can't be learned at boot camp!

4

JUSTICE AND FAIRNESS

*A strong sense of what's fair will help you
rise above personal disappointments.*

A lifelong friendship can begin as early as the fourth grade. That's what happened to Nathan and Peter. They were constant companions—and each other's biggest challenge—since that first meeting. Nathan's accomplishments became Peter's goals and vice versa. When one ran fast, the other one strove to run faster; when one got an A, the other one aimed for an A+. They were both athletic and smart, and their interests ran perfectly parallel to each other.

In high school they excelled at every sport. They were great team members. It seemed like one of them could tell where the other one would move or when he was going to throw the ball before that one knew it himself.

As a sophomore, Nathan began to consider an application to West Point. Both Nathan and Peter had become experts on the Civil War. Sharing books on the subject, they were fascinated that so many Civil War generals graduated from West Point but ended up on opposite sides during the conflict. The boys visited Gettysburg with their history class, and "Civil War Generals" became their favorite computer game.

Nathan shared everything with Peter, but for some reason he kept his personal interest in the academy to himself. Imagine Nathan's surprise when, near the end of their junior year, Peter announced that he was going to apply to West Point! Nathan was speechless. He didn't want Peter to think that his own desire to attend the military academy had anything to do with Peter's interest, but he knew it was time to tell the truth. "You're kidding." he began. "I requested information from West Point last year, and I've already contacted Representative Smith's office requesting a recommendation."

Peter hesitated. "Are you saying you don't want me to go for it?"

"Not at all," answered Nathan. "We'll both get in. What could be better than going through West Point with my best friend? And, if we don't, may the best man win."

As they shook hands on it, Peter had an idea. "Let's make a pact to open our acceptance letters together. After all, we have basically the

A career in the armed forces often includes the opportunity to travel to foreign countries.

same grades and the same interests. We're going to get in, which will be incredible, but if we are rejected, we'll cry on each other's shoulder. Agreed?"

"Agreed," Nathan replied, and each boy went about the process of obtaining admission to the highly selective school. Midway through their senior year the long-awaited letter arrived at Nathan's home, and he could barely keep from opening it. He couldn't go back on his word, however, so he told Peter the letter had arrived, set it on his desk, and waited for Peter to receive his notice. When it arrived a week later, Peter telephoned Nathan to let him know, picked up the important letter confidently, and met Nathan at their old childhood hideout behind the school. "Who goes first?" asked Peter. "Should we flip a coin?"

"Nah, lets just rip 'em open together."

"Woo-hoo!" Peter shouted a moment later. "We're in!"

"No, we're not," came the quiet, disappointed reply.

Peter couldn't believe it. How could it possibly be that he got in and Nathan didn't? They were so alike in every way. Heck, they were practically the same person. Peter threw his arm around Nathan's shoulder.

"It's okay. Hey, congratulations! I know you're going to become the most famous graduate of West Point ever," was Nathan's

People who value justice and fairness:

- treat all people the same (as much as possible).
- are open-minded; they are willing to listen to the points of views others and try to understand.
- consider carefully before making decisions that affect others.
- don't take advantage of others' mistakes.
- don't take more than their fair share.
- cooperate with others.
- recognize the uniqueness and value of each individual.
- don't get angry with others when circumstances do not go in their favor.

Adapted from material from the Character Counts Coalition, 4640 Admiralty Way, Suite 1001, Marina del Rey, California 90292.

Friendship and camaraderie knit soldiers together.

The Difference Between Right and Wrong

At the core, American citizen soldiers knew the difference between right and wrong, and they didn't want to live in a world in which wrong prevailed. So they fought and won, and we, all of us, living and yet to be born, must be forever profoundly grateful.
— Stephen E. Ambrose, discussing the American GIs in World War II

response, and the two young men embraced.

"What are you going to do now?" a concerned Peter asked.

"I'm going to try to get them to reconsider, and, if they don't, Plan B, I guess—ROTC." Nathan noticed the disappointment on Peter's face. "Hey, don't feel bad. Maybe I'll get in yet, and, if I don't, well, 'all's fair in love and war.' Isn't that what they say?"

Peter couldn't believe what a good sport Nathan was being. He was actually concerned about

The Medal of Honor is awarded to military personnel who demonstrate their sense of justice with acts of heroism and courage.

Thomas Paine's Thoughts on the Military

These are the times that try men's souls. The summer soldier and the sunshine patriot will, in this crisis, shrink from the service of his country; but he that stands it now, deserves the love and thanks of man and woman. Tyranny, like hell, is not easily conquered; yet we have this consolation with us, that the harder the conflict, the more glorious the triumph.

What would you do if you saw your friend treating someone unfairly?

- Would you immediately tell your friend to stop?
- Would you say something to your friend later?
- Would you walk away and pretend you didn't see what happened?
- Would you participate?
- Would you try to comfort the other person?

Peter's feelings. Peter wondered if he would be as gracious if he were in Nathan's place.

How would you feel if you were Nathan? Would you be jealous of your friend? Or would you be fair enough to genuinely wish the best for him? When life seems unjust, how do you respond? Do you possess a sense of justice and fairness that allows you to rise above personal disappointment?

Dreams and Goals

"I come before you this evening as a retired soldier, a fellow citizen who has lived the American Dream to its full, as one who believes in that dream and as one who wants that dream to come to a reality for every American. . . My sister and I were taught to believe in ourselves. We might be considered poor, but we were rich in spirit. We might be black and considered second-class citizens, but stick with it because we were Americans! Justice will eventually triumph and the powerful series of promises of the founding fathers will come true. We were taught by my parents—always, always, always believe in miracles!"

From Colin Powell's speech before Republican Delegates, 1996

Our vision first and foremost rests on values—values, because values are the conscience of a society. Values that must be lived, not just preached."

—*Colin Powell*

During the World War II battle at Iwo Jima, soldiers demonstrated an intense sense of responsibility to the flag. This statue at Arlington, Virginia, memorializes their bravery.

5

RESPONSIBILITY

*Our responsibilities in any given situation
are not always easy to determine—but
character demands we make the effort.*

Responsibility means being accountable for what we do. When we observe an injustice we have two choices. One is to act to stop the injustice; the other is to act in such a way as to allow the injustice to continue (by ignoring the situation, for example). In both cases we have performed an action, and in both cases we carry a responsibility for the results.

After a 30-year career in the military, Kenneth W. Johnson has some strong opinions regarding responsibility. He divides responsibility into two categories: static and dynamic. According to Mr. Johnson, "If I do what I and others know to be right and avoid doing what is wrong, I am responsible." Mr. Johnson defines this as static responsibility." In certain situations, however, the difference between right and wrong is not clearly defined. When individuals are called upon to make a decision in this type of situation, Mr. Johnson says they are engaged in "dynamic responsibility."

In 1990, U.S. Marine Corps Reserve Colonel Kenneth Johnson was called to active duty in Saudi Arabia during the Desert Storm campaign. While there he performed his static responsibilities as logistics plans officer by making sure soldiers had the food, water, ammunition,

During battle, soldiers are responsible for being alert and at their best.
The safety of their unit depends on each of them.

transportation, and medicine they needed. But earlier in his military career he had been forced to exercise dynamic responsibility, and the experience stuck with him to this very day.

In 1969, Rifle Platoon Commander Lieutenant Kenneth Johnson
was stationed in Vietnam. Although his platoon started out with 55
men, one third of them had been lost and several of the remaining soldiers were wounded. During a major campaign, a young marine was
discovered sleeping while on guard duty, an offense punishable by
death in times of war. The sergeant who made the discovery decided to
teach the sleeping marine a lesson by hitting him, a serious offense under military law. Lieutenant Johnson was faced with a serious decision:
Should he report these men?

According to Mr. Johnson, such a report could lead to ***court-
martials*** for both men. That would mean they'd be kicked out of the
military, and a dishonorable discharge like this can haunt an individual

According to the Six Pillars of Character. . .

- Beyond having the responsibility to be trustworthy, respectful, fair, and caring, ethical people show responsibility by being accountable, pursuing excellence, and exercising self-restraint.
- An accountable person does not shift blame or claim credit for the work of others.
- Responsible people finish what they start, overcoming rather than surrendering to obstacles and excuses.
- Responsible people exercise self-control, restraining passions and appetites for the sake of reason, prudence, and duty to set a good example.

During jungle warfare, character qualities like accountability and self-control are essential.

Accepting Responsibility

If you and a friend were caught passing notes to each other in class:
Would you blame your friend?
Would your friend blame you?
What if only your friend were caught? Would you step forward and claim your part of the responsibility?
If your friend asked to look at your paper during a test, what would you say?
What would you do if your friend looked at your test paper without asking permission? Would you ask him to stop? Would you tell your teacher?

for the rest of his or her life. Lieutenant Johnson realized that these men had made serious mistakes, but according to the law, he had discretion regarding their punishment. The platoon was already short on men, so the lives of the remaining soldiers would be in more jeopardy if these two were removed from active duty. Lieutenant Johnson was concerned, though, about what kind of message it would send to the troops if the men were not punished for their actions. After a discussion with them, the Lieutenant decided in favor of leniency and gave each of them another chance. Neither of the men committed another offense and the pla-

The battlefront will often require soldiers to have a sense of "dynamic responsibility."

Act Responsibly

Accountability: Think before you act. Consider the possible consequences on all people affected by actions. Think for the long-term. Be reliable. Accept responsibility for the consequences of your choices. Don't make excuses. Don't blame others for your mistakes or take credit for others' achievements. Set a good example for those who look up to you.

Pursue Excellence: Do your best with what you have. Keep trying; don't quit or give up easily. Be diligent and industrious.

From www.cortland.edu/c4n5rs/char_v.htm

Canadian peacekeeping troops have an enormous responsibility— preventing war.

> ### When the Consequences of Our Actions Are Not Clear
>
> I detest the term "friendly fire." Once a bullet leaves a muzzle or a rocket leaves an airplane, it is not friendly to anyone. . . . The very chaotic nature of the battlefield, where quick decisions make the difference between life and death, has resulted in numerous incidents of troops being killed by their own fires in every war this nation has ever fought. . . . Not even one such avoidable death should ever be acceptable.
> —General H. Norman Schwarzkopf

toon members' bonds seemed even stronger. In a speech made at Valley Forge Military Academy on April 8, 2001, Mr. Johnson explained that, "dynamic responsibility is the world of the military or business leader where the right answer is never self-evident, but the consequences may be immense."

As the bomb fell over Hiroshima and exploded, we saw an entire city disappear. I wrote in my log the words, "My God, what have we done?"

—Capt. Robert Lewis

General Eisenhower (portrayed by this statue) inspired the troops that served under his courageous leadership during World War II.

6

COURAGE

Courage gives you the strength to face the danger of battle—and it also empowers you to stand up for what is right.

June 6, 1944, D-Day: Normandy, France

The raging turmoil of the sea, the sound of battle, fear so palpable you could taste it within yourself and see it in your buddies crammed in the vessel with you—what courage it must have taken to leave the flat-bottomed landing boats and rush forward through the sea and onto the battlefield. Many of these young soldiers had never seen battle before. Though surrounded by others engaged in the same activity, each infantryman must have felt truly alone.

Soldiers landed on several beaches during the invasion, but the American First Division at Omaha Beach confronted the fiercest opposition. The Germans, well established on cliffs overlooking the beach, were able to sink many of the landing crafts miles from the shore. Some vessels carrying tanks were sunk, their crews trapped within them beneath the surface of the sea. Soldiers caught in strong sea currents floated up to two miles beyond their intended landing spots. After a fierce and deadly battle, the American *infantrymen* were able to take the beach. Soldiers did not die in vain, for with their surviving friends and comrades, they paved the way for thousands of troops and, eventually, for peace.

People who value courage:

- say what's right (even when no one agrees with them).
- do the right thing (even when it's hard).
- follow their conscience instead of the crowd.
- are willing to face danger for the sake of doing what is right for others.

Courage on the battlefield is one test of the human spirit, but the personal courage needed to face battles within oneself is just as compelling. Take the case of Senator Max Cleland (D-Georgia). Senator Cleland's personal journey took him from being voted "outstanding senior" in his high school class to college and then to Vietnam. In 1968, 25-year-old Max Cleland volunteered for one last, and as it turned out nearly fatal, mission in Vietnam, for during that mission Max Cleland was involved in an explosion that resulted in the loss of three of his limbs. Max Cleland's personal battle had begun, and it would take extreme courage to win. In his essay "Strong at the Broken Places" in *The Power of*

Our world today owes an enormous debt to the courage of the veterans who served in past wars.

Dwight D. Eisenhower

General Dwight D. Eisenhower's Orders to the Troops
Heading for D-Day, June 6, 1944, During World War II:

Soldiers, Sailors, and Airmen of the Allied Expeditionary Force—
You are about to embark on the Great Crusade toward
which we have striven these many months. The eyes of the
world are upon you. The hopes and prayers of liberty-loving
people everywhere march with you.

Your task will not be an easy one. Your enemy is well
trained, well equipped, and battle hardened. He will fight
savagely.

But this is the year 1944! . . . The tide has turned. The
free men of the world are marching together to Victory!

I have full confidence in your courage, devotion to duty,
and skill in battle. We will accept nothing less than full victory!

Character, Senator Cleland describes his emotions during the first days of his recovery as being like a roller coaster but says that after working through those emotions he came to realize, "I had to take the adversity I was facing and turn it into something positive. In search of purpose in my life, I turned to public service." The Senator explains that he has found both solace and inspiration in the empowering examples set by others. "What happens to us in our lives and how we face each challenge is what builds our character"—which, according to Max Cleland, is composed of "trustworthiness, respect, responsibility, fairness, caring, and citizenship." Max Cleland faced his personal battle with courage and determination and went on to become, at age 28, the youngest

A Poem Carried by Capt. John G. Burkhalter, a Participant in D-Day:

Be strong!
We are not here to play, to dream, to drift.
We have hard work to do and loads to lift.
Shun not the struggle,
face it: 'tis God's gift.

Be strong!
Say not the days are evil. Who's to blame?
And fold the hands and acquiesce, O shame!
Stand up, speak out
and bravely, in God's name.

Be strong!
It matters not how deep entrenched the wrong,
How hard the battle goes, the day is long:
Faint not, fight on!
Tomorrow comes the song.
    —by Maltbie D. Babcock

Sherman tanks were used to fight World War II.

Read About the Experiences of One Brave
D-Day Soldier in His Own Words:

Soon we are only 500 yards from the beach and are ordered to get down. Minutes later the boat stops and begins to toss in the waves. The ramp goes down and without hesitation my section leader, Cpl. John Gibson, jumps out well over his waist in water. He only makes a few yards and is killed. We have landed dead on into a pillbox with a machine gun blazing away at us. We didn't hesitate and jumped into the water one after the other—I was last of the first row. Where was everybody? My section are only half there—some were just floating on their Mae West's [life preservers].

—Jim Wilkin of the Queen's Own Rifles of Canada, B Company, describing his participation in the final wave assault on Juno Beach

Creed of the U.S. Army Infantry

I am the Infantry—Queen of Battle! For two centuries I have kept our Nation safe, purchasing freedom with my blood. To tyrants, I am the day of reckoning, to the suppressed, the hope for the future. Where the fighting is thick, there am I. I am the Infantry! FOLLOW ME!

I was there from the beginning, meeting the enemy face to face, will to will. My bleeding stained the snow at Valley Forge; my frozen hands pulled Washington across the Delaware. . . .

Where brave men fight, there fight I. In freedom's cause, I live, I die. From Concord Bridge to Heartbreak Ridge, from the Artic to the Mekong, to the Caribbean, the Queen of Battle! Always ready, then, now and forever. I am the Infantry! FOLLOW ME!

member of the Georgia State Senate before becoming a U.S. Senator in 1996. Columnist David Broden describes him as, "an authentic American hero, an inspiration to people everywhere, a living, breathing testament to the power of the human spirit."

Have you been called upon to exercise courage? Not everyone can leap from a boat while machine-gun fire rains down upon them, but everyone can find ways to exercise courage in their daily lives. Can you think of a time when you needed courage to overcome personal adversity? Was there a time when you did something you knew was right despite your fear? Have you developed a moral and ethical code in your personal life? Are you able to stand by your convictions even in the face of ridicule by others? If the answer to these questions is yes, you are on your way to becoming the best person you can be. Important, positive characteristics like courage will stand you well in either a military or a civilian career.

Above all, we must realize that no arsenal, or no weapon in the arsenals of the world, is so formidable as the will and moral courage of free men and women. It is a weapon our adversaries in today's world do not have."

—Ronald Reagan

Courage is doing what you're afraid to do. There can be no courage unless you're scared.

—Capt. Eddie Rickenbacker, World War I air ace

Members of the Special Forces need self-discipline and diligence to do their job.

7

SELF-DISCIPLINE AND DILIGENCE

*What lies behind us and what lies before
us are tiny matters compared to
what lies within us.*
—Ralph Waldo Emerson

A breed apart, a cut above the rest, another kind of soldier," these are some of the ways members of the U.S. Special Forces describe themselves. The U.S. Army, Navy, Air Force, and Marines all have Special Forces (sometimes called Elite Forces), but the best known are probably the Army Green Berets and the Navy Seals. Members of these elite forces possess great physical endurance and intelligence along with high moral and ethical character, self-discipline and diligence.

Bill Ellsworth first learned about the Special Forces while studying the story of the Vietnam War. He was impressed by the courage these soldiers demonstrated in the face of danger. They often conducted operations in small groups and sometimes deep within enemy territory. *In a situation like that, you really need to be able to rely on yourself and your buddies,* he thought.

Sometimes Bill wondered if he might have what it takes to become a member of a Special Forces "A" team. He knew they had to be diligent and decisive, since they often didn't have a lot of time to consider options before making decisions. Bill felt a little silly comparing life and death decisions to those he made as quarterback of the high school

During battle, Special Forces must be self-controlled, determined, and patient.

People who value self-discipline and diligence:

- work to control their emotions, words, actions, and impulses.
- give their best in all situations.
- keep going even when the going is rough.
- are determined and patient.
- try again even when they fail the first time.
- look for ways to do their work better.

Adapted from material from the Character Education Network (www.CharacterEd.Net).

football team, but he did select plays quickly, even when they were losing and game time was running out. Members of the team respected his judgment, because they realized Bill's decisions were based on a clear-headed evaluation of the situation. He made up his mind—and then he followed through.

Bill understood that self-discipline was another important trait, and he knew that was something he also possessed. During his freshman year, he had set his sights on becoming the valedictorian of his

Participating in a mass tactical parachute jump requires a unique brand of self-discipline.

class. After almost four years of self-disciplined study, he had reached his goal.

The Army agreed with Bill's evaluation of himself, and so it was that Bill eventually found himself in training that was more rigorous and intensive than he ever dreamed. It never stopped, even after he became a member of a Special Forces team, because the team stayed on constant alert. These soldiers never knew when or where their skills would be needed, so they constantly polished them and learned the use of new weapons. The men with whom Bill worked were the most impressive he had ever met. They never bragged about their abilities, but their abilities were in evidence every day. These men were of the highest moral character. Bill knew that when there was a secret to keep, they'd be able to keep it, and when there was danger, they'd be willing to look fear in the face.

Each member of Bill's team was trained in a specific area but cross-training to ensure that each member could handle multiple tasks was also important. Bill became a communications specialist, also called a

Rangers are specially trained in close-range fighting and raiding tactics.

Special Forces units use technology such as low-level voice interception.

Diligent attention to details is important when you're in the military. . .

A speck of dirt on your windscreen could turn into an enemy fighter in the time it took to look round and back again. A little smear on your goggles might hide the plane that was coming in to kill you.

—Derek Robinson, describing R.A.F. action in the Battle of France and the Battle of Britain in World War II

signaler. It would be Bill's job to operate a radio and also to call in any necessary **artillery** or air strikes.

The team was called into action in Afghanistan shortly after the War on Terrorism began. They traveled to Uzbekistan first and from there moved in and out of enemy territory. Their mountain climbing and rappelling training came in handy during their mission to find and destroy Taliban and al-Qaida forces in this rough and mountainous terrain. Surprise and speed were essential in these

AKMS assault rifles are among the weapons used by the Special Forces.

Medals of honor are awarded to military personnel whose diligence and courage are outstanding.

searches for occupied caves. A former Mujahedeen guerrilla, who had fought against the Russian occupation of Afghanistan in the 1980s and was now a member of the Northern Alliance, acted as guide and interpreter for the Special Forces team.

There were also about 700 Canadian troops under U.S. command in Afghanistan, mostly from the Canadian Special Forces known as the JTF2 (Joint Task Force 2). Bill met several members some of whom had served in Operation Harpoon, which involved about 400 Canadian troops leading an additional 100 Americans in the mountains of Afghanistan.

During the week of March 16, 2002, for the first time since 1953, Canadian troops killed enemy troops in combat. The last time was during the Korean War. There have been deaths during peacekeeping missions but none until now during combat situations.

All went well for Bill's team until the capture of several Afghan soldiers during a raid. Bill called in air strikes to destroy the cave where the soldiers had been captured, but the strikes began dangerously close to the Special Forces team and their prisoners. Moreover, one severely wounded prisoner slowed the team's exit from the area considerably. Not wanting to end up victims of "friendly fire," the thought of abandoning the prisoner in order to move more quickly crossed Bill's mind. He also thought about volunteering to take responsibility for the prisoner so the other members of his unit could leave the dangerous area more quickly, but that would put his own life in great peril . . . all to save a member of the enemy who might die from his wounds anyway.

What did self-discipline and diligence require of him in this situation? Bill only had a moment to make his decision.

What do you think he should do? What would you do if you were Bill? Have you ever had to make a choice between doing something to help yourself and making a sacrifice to help another person? Would you make a sacrifice even for a person you didn't like? Do you have the self-discipline to do the right thing—even when a part of you would rather not?

True happiness is not attained through self-gratification, but through fidelity to a worthy purpose.

—Helen Keller

Vietnam War soldiers (memorialized by this statue) fought for their country, demonstrating the character quality of citizenship.

8

CITIZENSHIP

Ask not what your country can do for you.
Ask what you can do for your country.
—John F. Kennedy

You never know what seemingly small event might alter the course
of your life. For Millie it was a book found on a picnic table in a
park. As she lifted the book she noticed the corner of one page had been
bent over to mark it. She turned to that page and read a short story that
altered her way of thinking forever, for that page held the secret of
Millie's purpose on the earth!

Millie read as a man recounted an incident of his youth. He had
been walking through a forest and noticed something shining on the
ground. It was a small piece of broken mirror. After casually putting it
in his pocket, he went on his way. From that day forward, when he
walked through the forest, as was his custom every day, he would take
the little sliver of mirror out and play with it. He was fascinated by the
way he could use it to point the sun into dark places in the forest. Over
time the little mirror came to embody a metaphor for the meaning of
life. He never knew what the entire mirror looked like, and that made
him think about the fact that he didn't really know what every aspect of
himself looked like. Even if he had the entire mirror and could see his
reflection in it, would it show him anything about his character? Would
it display anything about his integrity or his honesty or his values?

Would it reflect back to him the kind of person he was? No, but just as he could use the mirror to shine light into the dark places in the forest, he could use what he possessed and knew of himself to shine light into dark places in the world.

Millie felt her heart soar while reading that short tale. She placed the life-altering book back on the table, as she thought someone would certainly come to retrieve it, and she hoped other people might be lucky enough to stop and read the tattered pages.

Until this moment Millie had been in turmoil. She was about to graduate from college, and she had been offered a fantastic job. Well, she called it "fantastic" because a large salary was attached to it. There was just one problem: Millie didn't believe the company was an ethical one. She knew it had let a lot of workers go in the past few years because the company wasn't profitable. Now things were better, yet instead of hiring former employees back, the company was hiring new

Canadian and American soldiers who serve their countries may not make a lot of money—but some things are more important than financial gain.

Even young children can demonstrate citizenship and be role models for others:

There is a certain cemetery where some of my closest friends in the division lie. I saw it grow—shattered bodies lying there waiting for graves to be dug. Now it is filled. The graves are neat and trim, each with its cross. Occasionally I visit it when passing by. Always there are flowers on the graves: sometimes a potted geranium has been newly brought in; sometimes there is a handful of daisies. The French people, especially the children, seem to have charged themselves with this little attention.

From a letter written by a soldier sometime after D-Day.

Children left these tributes to the bravery of the Allied soldiers at D-Day.

People who value citizenship:

- play by the rules.
- obey the law.
- do their share.
- respect authority.
- stay informed about current events.
- vote.
- protect their neighbors and community.
- pay their taxes.
- give to others in their community who are in need.
- volunteer to help.
- protect the environment.
- conserve natural resources for the future.

Adapted from material from the Character Counts Coalition, 4640 Admiralty Way, Suite 1001, Marina del Rey, California 90292.

workers. The company was trying to save money, she supposed, because even though her salary offer was a generous one, it was less than what a worker with ten or 15 years of experience would be paid. The company must be saving thousands of dollars on employee benefits as well. She also disapproved of some of the company's business ventures. As a Native American, she had been raised to care about the environment, and this company made some of its money by exploiting the earth. *Is this what life's about?* she wondered. *Is making a lot of money all that's important?* She would love to have money, though. She had loans to pay back. This job would make it easy to do that. She'd even be able to send her parents on that trip to the Caribbean they'd been joking about, but she suspected really dreaming about, for the past ten years.

But some other thoughts had been creeping into Millie's mind lately. Hers was one of many countries whose armed forces were engaged in peacekeeping missions around the world. Millie had been thinking more and more about that sort of thing as she watched soldiers in foreign lands on the evening news. Maybe she should consider giving some of her time to her country. She had always felt lucky and proud of her citizenship, but she'd never really worked for it; freedom had been handed to her at birth. Maybe she owed something to her country.

But would she be a good soldier? It seemed strange to think of her-

As a member of the armed forces, you need to be clear about your values.

What Are Your Values?

Take the time to determine exactly what values are important to you. Your personal convictions, not those of others, will determine how you live.

To clarify your values ask yourself the following questions:

What do I believe in?

What governs my life?

What do I stand for?

What puts meaning into my life?

What qualities are important for my life to be complete?

In what guiding principles can I become constructively obsessed?

Excerpt from a speech given to ancient warriors by Thucydides in the 5th century B.C.:

Day by day fix your eyes upon the greatness of Athens, until you become filled with the love of her, and when you are impressed by the spectacle of her glory, reflect that this empire has been acquired by men who knew their duty and had the courage to do it.

self in the military. Could she afford to postpone civilian employment? Would she be able to find a job after getting out of the military? Was that even something she should concern herself with? Would she be happy in the military? Was it necessary for her to feel happiness? Maybe happiness comes from helping others.

Millie began to think about the passage in the book, and she began to wonder how best to shine her light into the dark places in the world.

Each person has a unique ability for shining light into the world's dark places.

The price of freedom is eternal vigilance."

—*Thomas Jefferson*

The infantry is just one of the many opportunities you can find in the armed forces.

9

CAREER OPPORTUNITIES

*Some people live an entire lifetime and
wonder if they ever made a difference
in the world, but the Marines don't
have that problem.*
—Ronald Reagan

Military personnel are stationed throughout the United States and
Canada and in many countries around the world. A wide variety
of occupational positions are available in the military. Each of them af-
fords the opportunity to develop and demonstrate positive character
traits while conducting important work for your country.

Enlisted personnel make up about 85 percent of the Armed Forces
and carry out the fundamental operations such as combat, administration, construction, engineering, healthcare, and human services. Officers make up the remaining 15 percent and are the leaders of the
military. They supervise and manage activities. Here are the major occupational groups for both enlisted personnel and officers.

Enlisted Occupational Groups

Administrative careers include a wide variety of positions. The military
must keep accurate information for planning and managing its operations. Records are kept on personnel, equipment, funds, supplies, and

other property. Administrative personnel record information, type reports, maintain files, and review information. Personnel may work in a specialized area such as finance, accounting, legal, maintenance, supply, or transportation. For example:

- Recruiting specialists recruit and place personnel and provide information about military careers to the public.
- Training specialists and instructors provide training programs necessary to help military personnel perform their jobs effectively.
- Personnel specialists collect and store information concerning training, job assignments, promotions, and health information.

Combat specialty occupations are positions whose members normally specialize by type of weapon system or combat operation.

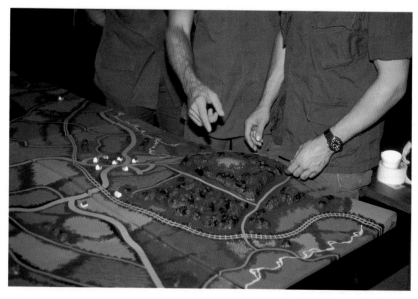

Combat specialists use terrain models to study tactical situations.

- Infantry and artillery are personnel that maneuver against enemy forces and position and fire artillery, guns, and missiles, and also operate tanks and amphibious assault vehicles.
- Special Forces operate weapons and execute special missions such as offensive raids, ***demolitions***, ***intelligence***, and search and rescue.

Construction occupations concern the building or repair of buildings, airfields, bridges, dams, bunkers, and electrical and plumbing components of these structures. Personnel operate bulldozers and other heavy equipment and work with engineers and other building specialists. Some specialize in certain areas.

- Plumbers and pipe fitters install and repair plumbing and pipe systems in buildings and on ships.
- Building electricians install and repair electrical wiring systems in offices, airplane hangars, and other buildings.

Electronic and electrical equipment repair personnel generally specialize by type of equipment, such as avionics, computer, optical, communications, or weapons systems.

- Electronic instrument repairers install, test, maintain, and repair electronic systems including navigational controls and biomedical instruments.
- Weapons maintenance technicians maintain and repair weapons, most of which have electronic components and systems that assist in locating targets and in aiming and firing weapons.

The military has many engineering, science, and technical occupations whose members operate technical equipment, solve complex problems, or provide and interpret information. Enlisted personnel normally specialize in one area such as space operations, emergency management, environmental health and safety, or intelligence.

- Space operations specialists use and repair spacecraft ground control command equipment.
- Emergency management specialists prepare emergency procedures for disasters such as floods, tornadoes, and earthquakes.
- Environmental health and safety specialists inspect military facilities and food supplies for conditions hazardous to health and the environment.
- Intelligence specialists gather and study information using aerial photographs and various types of radar and surveillance systems.

Military Oath of Enlistment

I do solemnly swear that I will support and defend the Constitution of the United States against all enemies, foreign and domestic; that I will bear true faith and allegiance to the same; and that I will obey the orders of the President of the United States and the orders of the officers appointed over me, according to regulations and the Uniform Code of Military Justice. So help me God.

Healthcare personnel assist medical professionals in treating men and women in the military. They may work in close contact with doctors, dentists, nurses, and physical therapists within a hospital or clinic. Healthcare specialists normally specialize in a particular area. They may provide emergency medical treatment, operate diagnostic equipment, conduct laboratory tests, maintain pharmacy supplies, or maintain patient records.

Human services specialists help military personnel and their families with social or personal problems, or assist chaplains.

- Caseworkers and counselors work with personnel who may be experiencing social problems, drug or alcohol dependence, or depression.
- Religious program specialists assist chaplains with religious programs and administrative duties.

Machine operator and production occupations personnel operate industrial equipment and tools to fabricate and repair parts for a variety of items and structures. They may operate engines, turbines, nuclear reactors, or water pumps. Personnel often specialize by type of work performed.

- Welders and metal workers repair or form the structural parts of ships, submarines, buildings, or other equipment.
- Survival equipment specialists inspect, maintain, and repair parachutes, aircraft life support equipment, and so on.
- Dental and optical laboratory technicians construct and repair dental equipment and eyeglasses.

Media and public affairs personnel are involved in the public presentation and interpretation of information and events. They take and develop photographs; film, record, and edit audio and video programs; present news and music programs; and produce graphic artwork, drawings, and other visual displays. Other public affairs specialists act as interpreters and translators.

The airborne qualification badge means its wearer is entitled to fly.

Transportation specialists may pilot helicopters.

Service personnel enforce military laws and regulations, provide emergency response to disasters, and maintain food standards. Personnel normally specialize by function.

- Military police control traffic, prevent crime, and respond to emergencies.
- Other law enforcement and security specialists investigate crimes committed on military property and guard inmates in military facilities.
- Firefighters put out, control, and help prevent fires in buildings, on aircraft, and aboard ships.
- Food service specialists prepare food in dining halls, in hospitals, and on board ships.

Transportation and material handling specialists ensure the safe transport of people and cargo. Most personnel within this group are classified according to mode of transportation:

- Aircrew members operate equipment on board aircraft.
- Vehicle drivers operate all types of heavy military vehicles including fuel and water trucks, semi-tractor trailers, heavy troop transports, and passenger buses.
- Quartermasters and boat operators navigate and pilot many types of small watercraft including tugboats, gunboats, and barges.
- Cargo specialists load and unload military supplies using equipment such as forklifts and cranes.

Vehicle and machinery mechanics conduct preventive and corrective maintenance on aircraft, ships, automotive and heavy equipment, heating and cooling systems, marine engines, and powerhouse station equipment. They typically specialize by the type of equipment.

- Aircraft mechanics work on helicopters and airplanes.
- Automotive and heavy equipment mechanics work on jeeps, cars, trucks, tanks, self-propelled missile launchers, other combat vehicles, and also bulldozers, power shovels, and other construction equipment.
- Heating and cooling mechanics use their skills to keep air-conditioning, refrigeration, and heating equipment working well.
- Marine engine mechanics keep gasoline and diesel engines on ships, boats, and other watercraft, and shipboard mechanical and electrical equipment running smoothly.
- Powerhouse mechanics work on electrical and mechanical equipment in power-generating stations.

Officer Occupational Groups

Combat specialty officers plan and direct military operations, oversee combat activities, and serve as combat leaders. This category includes officers in charge of tanks and other armored assault vehicles, artillery systems, Special Operations Forces, and infantry. They normally specialize by type of unit that they lead. Within the unit, they may specialize by the type of weapon system. For example:

- Artillery and missile system officers direct personnel as they target, launch, test, and maintain various types of missiles and artillery.
- Special Operations officers lead units in offensive raids, demolitions, intelligence gathering, and search and rescue missions.

Engineering, science, and technical officers have a wide range of responsibilities based on area of expertise. They lead or perform activities in areas such as space operations, environmental health and safety, and engineering. These officers may direct the operations of communications centers or the development of complex computer systems.

- Environmental health and safety officers study air, ground, and water to identify and analyze sources of pollution and its effects, and direct programs to control safety and health hazards in the workplace.
- Aerospace engineers design and direct the development of military aircraft, missiles, and spacecraft.

Executive, administrative, and managerial officers oversee and direct activities in areas such as finance, accounting, health administration, international relations, and supply.

- Health services administrators are responsible for the overall quality of care provided at the hospitals and clinics they operate and must ensure that each department works together to provide the highest quality of care.
- Purchasing and contracting managers negotiate and monitor contracts for billions of dollars worth of equipment, supplies, and services purchased from private industry.

Healthcare officers provide services based on their area of specialization. Officers who assist in examining, diagnosing, and treating patients include physician assistants and registered nurses. Other healthcare officers provide therapy, rehabilitative treatment, and other services:

- Physical and occupational therapists plan and administer therapy to help patients adjust to disabilities, regain independence, and return to work.
- Speech therapists evaluate and treat hearing and speech problems.
- Dietitians manage food service facilities and plan meals for hospital patients and for outpatients on special diets.
- Pharmacists manage the purchasing, storing, and dispensing of medicine.

Military Salaries

In general, full-time members of the U.S. military are paid a starting wage that is approximately 44 percent of what they would receive in a similar civilian position. Members of the military receive benefits (food and shelter, for example), which act as a supplement to their salaries. For each year of service in the military, a salary increase of 3 percent is received. An increase in major rank can raise a soldier's wages by 50 percent.

Health diagnosing and treating practitioner officers examine, diagnose, and provide treatment for illnesses, injuries, and disorders.

- Physicians and surgeons provide the majority of medical services to the military and their families.
- Dentists treat diseases and disorders of the mouth.
- Optometrists treat vision problems by prescribing eyeglasses and contact lenses.
- Psychologists provide mental healthcare and conduct research on behavior and emotions.

Human services officers perform services in support of the morale and well-being of military personnel and their families.

- Social workers focus on improving conditions that cause social problems such as alcohol abuse, racism, and sexism.
- Chaplains conduct worship services and perform other spiritual duties.

Media and public affairs officers oversee the development, production, and presentation of information or events for the public. They may produce and direct motion pictures, videotapes, and television and radio broadcasts that are used for training, news, and entertainment. Some plan, develop, and direct military bands.

Transportation occupations officers manage activities related to the safe transport of personnel and material by air and water. Officers normally specialize by mode of transportation or area of expertise because, in many cases, they must meet licensing and certification requirements:

- Pilots fly various types of specialized airplanes and helicopters to carry troops and equipment and execute combat missions.
- Navigators use radar, radio, and other equipment to determine their position and plan their route of travel.
- Officers on ships and submarines manage various departments aboard vessels.
- Ship engineers direct engineering departments aboard ships and submarines, including engine operations, maintenance, repair, heating, and power generation.

Training received in the military transfers well into civilian life. Many military personnel in the United States retire with a pension after 20 years of service and begin a civilian career. More than 365,000 U.S. personnel must be recruited each year to replace those who complete their commitment or retire. You can make a positive difference in the world through a military or a civilian career. Work hard, study hard, and above all, never forget that your character counts!

More Important Than Money

Advancements and salary raises are achievements valued by any professional. But being in the military means far more than any degree, title, or salary figure. The ability to make the world a better place can't be measured. "There were other opportunities, making a lot more money than I am now," admits General Colin Powell. "Every time I have faced up to this choice, I just find the satisfaction of being a soldier and the love of my profession overwhelming and more important to me than making a great deal of money or doing something I may not like as much as being a soldier."

Therefore I say: "Know your enemy and know yourself; in a hundred battles you will never be in peril."

—*Sun Tzu, The Art of War (c. 490 B.C.)*

FURTHER READING

Josephson, Michael, and Hanson, Wes. *The Power of Character.* San Francisco: Jossey-Bass Publishers, 1998.

Kidder, Rushworth M. *How Good People Make Tough Choices.* New York: Simon & Schuster, 1995.

McNab, Chris. *The World's Best Soldiers.* Broomall, Penn.: Mason Crest Publishers, 2003.

Paradis, Adrian *Opportunities in Military Careers.* Lincolnwood, Ill.: VGM Career Horizons Publishing Group, 1999.

Sheafer, Silvia Anne. *Women in America's Wars.* Springfield, N.J.: Enslow Publishers, 1996.

Smith, Robert Barr. *Men at War: True Stories of Heroism and Honor.* New York: Avon, 1997.

For Additional Information

Center for the 4th and 5th Rs
www.cortland.edu/c4n5rs

Character Counts
www.charactercounts.org

Character Education Network
www.charactered.net

Josephson Institute of Ethics
www.josephsoninstitute.org

U.S. Army
www.goarmy.com

U.S. Navy Seals
www.navyseals.com

Publisher's Note:

The Web sites on this page were active at the time of publication. The publisher is not responsible for Web sites that have changed their address or discontinued operation since the date of publication. The publisher will review and update the Web sites upon each reprint.

GLOSSARY

Artillery The branch of the army that uses mounted firearms and missiles.

Court-martials Trials for members of the armed forces; commissioned officers act as the judges.

Demolitions Destruction of buildings, roads, or bridges using explosives.

Deployed Placed in battle formation.

Empathy The ability to feel another's pain or suffering.

Holocaust The mass slaughter of civilians, especially Jews, by the Nazis during World War II.

Infantrymen Soldiers trained to fight on foot.

Intelligence Information concerning the enemy.

Recruiting Enlisting or enrolling in the armed services.

Recruits Soldiers who recently enlisted or were drafted.

Seizures Sudden, usually neurological attacks that may cause a person to lose muscle control.

Yarmulke A skullcap worn by Orthodox and Conservative male Jews.

INDEX

BIOGRAPHIES

Joyce Libal is a graduate of the University of Wisconsin, Green Bay. She lives and works as a magazine editor in Northeastern Pennsylvania.

Cheryl Gholar is a Community and Economic Development Educator with the University of Illinois Extension. She has a Ph.D. in Educational Leadership and Policy Studies from Loyola University, and she has more than 20 years of experience with the Chicago Public Schools as a teacher, counselor, guidance coordinator, and administrator. Recognized for her expertise in the field of character education, Dr. Gholar assisted in developing the K–12 Character Education Curriculum for the Chicago Public Schools, and she is a five-year participant in the White House Conference on Character Building for a Democratic and Civil Society. The recipient of numerous awards, she is also the author of *Beyond Rhetoric and Rainbows: A Journey to the Place Where Learning Lives.*

Ernestine G. Riggs is an Assistant Professor at Loyola University Chicago and a Senior Program Consultant for the North Central Regional Educational Laboratory. She has a Ph.D. in Educational Leadership and Policy Studies from Loyola University, and she has been involved in the field of education for more than 35 years. An advocate of teaching the whole child, she is a frequent presenter at district and national conferences; she also serves as a consultant for several state boards of education. Dr. Riggs has received many citations, including an award from the United States Department of Defense Overseas Schools for Outstanding Elementary Teacher of America.